COUPLE SKILLS

Proven Strategies to Improve Your Relationship by Unlocking One Another and Becoming Better Partners

Heather Miller

Photo credits:
KS kelly_sikkema
AS annie-spratt

Table of Contents

Introduction

Relationships can be a lot of work. They can be demanding, nerve-wracking and hurtful. They require love, care, understanding, and appreciation. This book aims to help you understand yours and take whatever necessary measures it requires to keep it enriched and nourished. Keep in mind that only you and your partner have to do all the work as a team. We are all born with the need to be loved, which also describes our humanity in a nutshell. That need is never outgrown and rarely underestimated, as most of us spend years of our lives searching for "the one." Love is not enough, although romance novels and romantic comedies are trying to propagate the idea that a couple will stay together if they are truly in love with each other no matter what. "Love" and "being in love," however, are different—the first takes effort, dedication, commitment, appreciation, acceptance, recognition, honesty, trust, communication, readiness to forgive, and support the loved one. Our guide is created and designed based on careful research and collective experiences noted in different types of relationships, so you and your partner could utilize this book as the first aid for relationship growth and development.

A healthy and consistent conversation is the cornerstone of every relationship. It is the glue that holds the relationship together. A lack of it can ruin even the most perfect of couples. Therefore, to lead a blissful and pleasant life, communication must be improved.

Lucky for you, in this book, we tackle some of the biggest and most common challenges couples face. If you're reading this book, you are likely looking to either improve relationships or find new relationships that are unhealthy.

Relationships are built not only on love but the science behind it as well. We will learn about fundamental lessons that are simple but difficult to master. At the same time, we will look at the bases of relationships and how communication can improve them.

Happy Reading.

Chapter 1: To Live in a Happy Relationship, You Must Acquire "Skills" That Will

Make Your Relationship Stable, Happy and Lasting

What Is a Heart-Centered Relationship?

Respect

Never calling your partner names, belittling them, or undermining the value of what they believe and do. Taking their projects seriously and valuing their insight and input during conversations. A respected partner is not necessarily one that you always agree with, only respecting their ability to hold different opinions.

Honesty

Without trust, there can be no real depth of connection. Honest partners go above and beyond simply refraining from lying, they actively try to be transparent with their partners, communicating their experience and not hiding things that their partner would prefer to know.

Trust

On the flip side, relationships with heart do not operate with mistrust and suspicion. In a healthy partnership, someone is innocent until proven guilty. Trust is given freely and not as some sort of reward or bonus. Partners assume the best of each other and do not need to snoop on them or demand they prove their loyalty.

Encouragement

The right partner will love to see you happy and successful. They'll push you to be the best version of yourself because they believe in you. This kind of love is selfless—such a partner cares about what you're doing with your life for no reason other than that they want you to live well. Partners who are each other's cheerleaders will never be alone when it comes to weathering life's difficulties.

Communication

It's a key to success in all aspects of your life and a romantic relationship is no exception. Communication involves expressing feelings for one another, giving each other compliments, or showing gratitude. Furthermore, it is important to discuss and debate different problems in your relationship rather than sweeping them under a rug. Improving communication with your partner is the first and most important thing you have to build a strong relationship.

Quality Over Quantity

Most couples want to spend as much time as possible together. However, that isn't always the definition of a successful relationship. The quality of time spent together is more important than how much time it is. Therefore, you should always strive to do something meaningful that makes you and your significant other happy. You can do various couple activities, travel, go to a restaurant, go to a football game or a concert, etc.

Time Apart

While you love spending time with your partner, always remember that both you and he/she need to spend some time apart as well. Being able to do what you love and retain your independence is vital for the relationship. After all, maintaining some boundaries that support each other's autonomy and independence is a key to a long-lasting relationship.

Different Love Languages

Gary D. Chapman, a relationship counselor and author of "The 5 Love Languages" came up with the idea that both men and women have five love languages i.e. unique ways of feeling love. These languages are:

- Receiving gifts
- Affirmation
- Quality time
- Acts of service
- Physical touch.

It is highly important to know which one of these languages speaks to you along with your partner. Telling each other what makes you feel loved the most is crucial for establishing a strong relationship and a healthy connection with your partner.

Appreciation

Showing how much you appreciate someone just for being in your life is very important. Although you know they are aware of how much you appreciate them, it is still very important to express those feelings. Appreciation can also be expressed through gestures, such as acts of kindness, getting flowers, etc.

Positive vs. Negative Qualities

When dealing with stressful situations or other events that anger us, we usually tend to observe the entire world from a negative perspective, including our partners. Sometimes, everything he or she does is perceived as negative in our eyes. Of course, there is always something about them you don't like. For example, you might not like their favorite show or the way they chew their food, etc. But, instead of focusing on things you don't like and let them pile on, you should focus on things you do like. It's important to opt for positive rather than negative qualities at all times. Also, you should bear in mind that their tiny imperfections are the qualities that make them who they are and you love that person.

Choosing Battles

Every relationship includes disagreements and arguments from time to time. They are inevitable. However, instead of reacting angrily to everything that bothers you, you should choose your battles wisely and only engage in arguments that are worth arguing. For example, it's not useful to have a big argument over the fact that he or she used your favorite coffee cup.

Sex

We have already established that healthy sex life is key to building intimacy, physical and emotional. Sex is an amazing way of connecting to someone on a deeper well. The more you get it, the more you want it. Happy couples know that regular sex life and keeping the spark alive are crucial for a strong relationship. You should also try to spice things up from time to time. Dare to experiment.

Don't Compare

The worst thing you do to your partner, besides cheating them, is to constantly compare them to your previous partners and wives/husbands of your friends. You also tend to compare your own life with someone else's. Comparing isn't healthy. People move through different life stages at different rates. Instead of trying to compare with someone else, you should appreciate what you already have.

Variety And Spontaneity

It's easy to be endlessly fascinated with your partner in the early days. Later on, when they are less of a mystery to you, you'll both need to take deliberate actions to maintain the proverbial spice of life. Routine is death for a relationship. In a strong, healthy relationship, both partners constantly strive to try new things, go places, learn things and rediscover their partner over and over again. It may sound like a bit of a paradox, but spontaneity is something that can be planned and controlled!

Pillars to a Successful Happy Marriage

Practice Positive Focus through Appreciation and Gratitude

Making sure to perceive things you like about your partner just as things that cause you to feel thankful for them may appear insignificant, yet gratefulness and gratitude act like super paste for a marriage.

Make Room for Fun

Fun is one of the main setbacks of married life. Regularly, when a couple gets hitched, their life rapidly moves toward becoming overpowered with working, paying bills, keeping up the house, and attempting to make space for time to rest. This issue is perplexed if the couple has youngsters. Frequently, the consequence of this expansion in stress is that fun-loving nature vanishes from the relationship. Wedded couples should search for ways to have a fabulous time, joke, and be energetic together along these lines.

Be a Partner in Good just as in Bad

Our partners furnish us with help when we are battling. This help is, in fact, one of the most significant advantages of marriage. Be that as it may, regularly, this is all marriage progresses toward becoming. Partners share bad times yet not good times. Partners who react energetically to each other's victory by posing inquiries, paying compliments, and offering support, experience more noteworthy relationship satisfaction after some time.

Allow Your Partner to Change

Giving your partner, just like yourself, a chance to change is crucial to continue your relationship. The more significant part of us gets so acquainted with our partners that we stop seeing them. In any case, the fact that you have quit seeing them doesn't mean they've abandoned evolving. Believing that it is conceivable ever genuinely to know anybody, including your companion, is a lie.

Practice Random Acts of Kindness

A standout amongst the best ways to show love and backing to your partner is to perform random acts of kindness. Random acts of kindness are remotely focused shows of love. These acts can be both unconstrained and arranged. They can come in numerous structures, such as gift, administration, real fondness, positive words, or unified time and consideration.

Practice the Art of Healthy Communication

Healthy communication in a marriage takes a goal and a lot of practice. It is almost painful to determine clashes between one another or keep up a genuine, getting partnership without communication. The heart of each argument between couples emerges from the inability to perceive the base of evidence itself.

The School of Honesty

Sometimes, honesty is the hardest part of discussing emotional issues with your spouse, but regardless of the expected repercussion, always dare to practice honesty. What has been hidden in the dark will surely come to light. Always be the one to bring it into the open. Do not allow circumstances to expose your lies.

Just Hear Them Out

Some of our spouses are bad at choosing the time to have an emotional conversation that sometimes you feel an immediate irritation when they begin to talk about their feelings. Since you don't have to say anything, you don't have to feel irritated or shut them up anyway.

Just be patient enough to hear them out. The opportunities they see to talk to you might not be the opportunity you see. Always allow them to finish talking and you can make time for yourself to respond when you are less irritated and have fully analyzed the issue they brought to the table.

Working Together

A marriage is a partnership for life. You are together, you do things together, everything about your life is now about the both of you. There are good times, there are bad, but you will always be going through it together. This is why communication, honesty, and trust are the three key factors in any marriage. Yes, there are other parts, like sex, that are important too, but these are the three things that will always make or break a successful marriage and should never be neglected—they are something to strive for.

But working as a team doesn't mean doing every activity together. Instead, teamwork in a relationship is about recognizing each other for what you are—your strengths, your differences, and everything in between. Use and help each other to solve your problems instead of relying on just one of you. Make use of each other's strong points and support their weaker ones. A lot of people call their partner their "other half." Well, why do you think that is? Keep it in mind.

On the other hand, coming back to arguments and decisions, in general, should be done together. Always. Big decisions come around more often than you might expect and it's important to make them together. Take your time to think about it, discuss it and then, make a move. Even if it doesn't affect them in any way, they must be involved in making that decision.

But teamwork doesn't work alone. Trust and honesty are the bedrock of all strong and healthy relationships—if you can't trust one another, then nothing will work. You need to understand each other's wants and needs and trust each other to fulfill them. You need to trust that your partner can do what needs to be done to support you and they need to feel the same about you.

Healing the Pain of the Past

Your road to overcoming fear of intimacy includes one important aspect – making peace with the past.

Although letting go of the past and making peace with everything that occurred back then seems impossible to you, the good thing is—it can be accomplished. Remember, past experiences should be taken as lessons you can learn from, instead of failures that sabotage you. When you look at everything that happened in childhood or past relationships as lessons, you will get a whole new perspective on the present and future. A good thing about bad experiences from the past is that you know how to avoid them now. Isn't that accomplishment by itself? Of course, it is. Taking the situation to learn, build on it, and avoiding it is already a form of success as it shows you're on the right track.

Inability to process adequately bad experiences when they occur can impact our relationships with people in the future. I have already mentioned how negative experiences affect us and stressed the importance of dealing with them properly when they occur. But, just because others didn't notice emotional distress in childhood or if you refused to admit how you felt and process emotions whenever something bad happened, it doesn't mean you can't make peace with the past and let it go. Below, you can see important facts that will help you do so:

Memories aren't the problem – memory is just a thought and has no power to destroy your capability to love and establish an intimate connection with someone. However, some thoughts are "sticky." It usually happens when you think of some bad experience and continue to dwell on it so much it ruins your perspective of how relationships with other people should be like. It's important to realize it's not good to repeat these sticky thoughts—they bring nothing to the table.

Accept that things happened for a reason, good or bad. Also, bear in mind that your past led you to this moment in the present when you finally have the opportunity to work on having the relationship you deserve.

Trying to forget past experiences doesn't lead anywhere. It's in your memory already. Instead, the ultimate victory is to neutralize it so the memory of a past bad experience doesn't have power over you, e.g., to stop feeling bad about yourself whenever you think of it.

The path to healing and making peace with the past occurs when you are fed up with how past experiences affect you now, ages after they happened.

To release the past, it is important to take responsibility either for situations that occurred or for allowing those events to control you.

Feeding negative or "limiting" thoughts only aggravates the entire process. Instead, whenever you start thinking of past experiences and how you don't want the same scenario to happen, you should immediately think of something encouraging. You have learned from your experience and you are smart enough to avoid the same mistake or same event.

Remembering that past experiences don't define you, and finally finding out who you are is the ultimate sign of freedom (and you deserve it).

Moving on from a Past Relationship

Past relationships have a big impact on our attitude in future relationships, particularly if they ended badly. When you were betrayed or cheated on in the past, you tend to think that all men or women are the same, so you are afraid of connecting to other people on a more emotional level. Due to bad relationships from the past, you can be afraid of intimacy and push your significant other away so you don't have to go through rejection. Below, you can see how successfully move on from a past relationship and improve your current or future bond with someone who deserves you:

- Accept that you were happy in that particular relationship, but it came to end; acceptance is a form of closure.
- Keep in mind that people are different and they do different things. Just because your boyfriend or girlfriend did something bad in the past, it doesn't mean the current or future one will do the same.
- Never compare your significant other to someone from your past.
- Remember that our relationships don't define us.

- If they didn't realize what you had to offer, it's their loss, not yours.
- Reflect on what went wrong to analyze not only the breakup but your attitude to be emotionally connected with your significant other.
- Learn to forgive and let go.
- Don't give your power away. The pain you felt was inevitable, but choosing to suffer is optional.
- Never punish your significant other for things that someone from your past did.
- Don't dwell on negative experiences and bad relationships. Instead, use them as lessons and focus on all good things that happened and are still happening. One bad relationship should not overrule multiple good ones.
- You can't change things that happened in the past, but you can change your perspective and respond to them.
- Don't be afraid to talk to your significant other about your bad experiences (romantic and non-romantic ones). This isn't comparing them to other people. Here, you're just letting them know why you find it difficult to relax. Being honest with your

significant other is very important. Plus, they will know you are interested, but struggling, and they'll help you get over your problem effectively.

Chapter 2: Understand the Emotions in a Relationship and Know How to Adapt Them to Each Situation

Negative Emotions

Jealousy

Most people who experience jealousy in relationships mistake it for love. After all, you are only trying to protect your relationship, or are you? This is not just a fallacy but jealousy has the exact opposite effect of protecting your relationship. Jealousy is a destructive emotion that undermines trust in relationships. It feeds anxiety and drains all the joy from your relationship.

Jealousy is driven by insecurity and fear. When you are afraid of losing someone, you see potential threats everywhere. You get jealous of their relationship with their friends, family, or even siblings. You assume everyone is trying to get at your partner or break your relationship. The problem with jealousy is that it is based on irrational thoughts that lead to irrational behavior more often than not.

Anger

Have you ever unleashed a tirade against your partner for something as petty as where he left the toothpaste? Most couples will tell you that their fights started over small things that should not matter in the general scheme of things. When we start letting negative emotions fester, gradually, small issues become big open wounds and, before you know it, you are full of rage and have angry outbursts at the drop of a hat.

Anger is a destructive emotion that makes you want to lash out and hurt your partner. When you feel aggrieved by your partner somehow, you feel the need to hurt them in return. Anger can be one of the most destructive negative emotions in relationships. It can lead to aggressive behavior and fuel feelings of hatred and animosity.

Revenge

Wanting to get even is a natural human instinct. People feel the need to settle scores to heal from a grievance that was meted out on them. While this may work in sports and other competitions, revenge in relationships is destructive and usually the beginning of the end.

Your partner cheated so you want to have an affair of your own to even the score. He said hurtful things so you say hurtful things back to make him hurt as much as you did. Whatever grievance is that you feel the need to revenge, when you allow this negative emotion to take root in your relationship, you will not have a relationship for long.

Fear

Behind every dysfunctional relationship is an element of fear. Fear is a powerful emotion that affects how you think and act. When fear drives you, your sole purpose comes down to neutralize the perceived threat whether real or imaginary.

If you fear abandonment, you will find yourself forgoing your own needs to keep your partner happy. This is because you want to keep them in the relationship at all costs. This unequal dynamic creates a relationship where one person is giving too much and getting little in return. In this situation, your resentment starts to build and you find yourself in a constant state of anxiety.

Poor Communication

The number one reason relationships break down is communication breakdown. Technology may have come very far, but there is still no alternative to communicating with your partner to know what they are feeling. When people cannot express themselves openly and freely in a relationship, it becomes impossible to be on the same page.

Real communication goes beyond just talking. It involves everything from tone of voice, body language, and other nonverbal cues. Sometimes, you can read much more into how someone feels through how they say things than the words that are coming out of their mouth. When the communication in your relationship is characterized by bickering, passive-aggressive behavior, or even silent treatment, the distance between you and your partner grows greater every day.

Communicating Through Intense Emotion

Getting to the Root of Your Feelings

There are quite a few reasons why you may be upset or arguing with your partner. You can't solve your problem if you do not even know what it is. Here are some common feelings and issues that can spark these arguments or overwhelming emotions:

Jealousy. While feeling jealous of your partner sometimes is natural, too much of it can lead to being possessive or territorial. Eventually, you can drive your partner away if you do not sit down and recognize why you feel so jealous. Dr. Susan Krauss Whitbourne takes us through the process of easing feelings of envy and jealousy by taking us through these questions and tips.

Insecurity. Feeling down about your self-image reflects how you behave and how you speak to your partner. You tend to become more pessimistic and look for reasons that your partner may not love you anymore when that simply is not the case. If you find yourself thinking things like, "I'm not good enough," dissipate those ugly lines of thinking with logical reasoning. Remind yourself of all the good times you and your spouse or boyfriend/girlfriend have had. Listen to the compliments they pay you and reflect on those instead of moping.

Feeling Unsatisfied. Maybe your relationship has been stuck in a rut lately. Things aren't exactly great in the bedroom and you two have hit a routine that feels monotonous. Feeling unsatisfied with your love life can be frustrating and you come to resent your partner.

Your Feelings May Be Unrelated Entirely to the goings-on in your relationship. Stress that comes from work or anger from tensions with a friend can bleed into your romantic life. Your built-up emotions spill out because you want to vent, but it comes out the wrong way.

Exercising Self Control

If you have any hope of keeping your emotions in check throughout the argument or discussion, you absolutely must have a solid measure of self-control. This may mean learning to hold your tongue when all you want to do is scream at your significant other and take out all of your negative feelings on them. If you are still reading, you know by now that doing this is what probably got you here in the first place. I know that resisting the temptation just to go berserk is hard, sometimes *really* hard. So what should you do when that urge arises?

1.) Reward yourself for good behavior. Whenever you fight the irrational anger and win, treat yourself to a snack. The next time the tense situation arises, your brain will subconsciously really want that snack later, so it will encourage you not to let your ego out of its cage. Progressively make your rewards for yourself bigger until your desire to fly off the handle is diminished completely.

2.) Monitor yourself and notice behavioral patterns. What is it, exactly, that sets you off in emotionally charged discussions? Is there a phrase, facial expression, or tone that your partner uses that just really enrages or upsets you? If you notice it, talk to them about it or avoid bringing up anything of that topic unless it is important enough to warrant a serious talk.

3.) Set goals for yourself. Something like, "I will not raise my voice with my significant other this week," is a good place to start, and you can build up over time. Do not punish yourself too hard when you fail, but refrain from doing anything your brain could mistake as a reward. We all mess up, but we shouldn't let ourselves get our mistakes too often or become regular behavioral patterns again.

These are small ways to help yourself that drastically change the future of your willpower. Now, you can focus on coping with your stress and know that you can stick to the strategies without throwing caution to the wind.

Coping Mechanisms During Times of Stress

We have all been there—we struggle to remain calm when a certain argument or discussion has us all choked up. Fighting tears or anger while speaking to a partner is difficult, I know. There is a simple scientific explanation for the awful way you feel when your emotions get intense, and you can override those feelings with a few coping mechanisms.

When you get upset or anxious, your sympathetic nervous system starts working overtime. Your heart rate shoots up, your temperature rises, a heavy feeling settles in your chest and you feel like your throat is closing up. These symptoms are all because of our "fight or flight" response. But why does it flare up in situations where we are not in actual danger?

Instead of running or fighting with your partner, though, use some coping tips to take a pause, calm down and reenter the conversation with a clear and rational mind.

Pace your breathing! Doing breathing exercises will counteract the symptoms of your "fight or flight" response. Breathe in through your nose for about four seconds, hold it for two and release through the mouth for five seconds. Hold your breath again for a couple of seconds and repeat about six times. The purpose of this exercise is to slow your heart rate, making your entire body relax.

Lower your expectations. You may be a perfectionist, and you want everything to come out exactly the way you pictured it. The truth is that no situation will turn out exactly according to plan. Your partner will not often react the way you want them to, so try not to overthink and over plan what you will say or do.

Avoid the situations that will cause an emotional flare-up. If you know that your partner will be angry if you bring up a serious topic in the car, wait until you get home to talk about it.

Only talk about what you know you can handle. If something is still too overwhelming and will spin your emotions out of control, give yourself more time to think about it.

Change the way you think about a problem. Instead of dwelling on the negative, think about all the ways your life could go right if you move past your difficult emotions. Changing your thoughts and reinforcing them with positive thoughts and hope will motivate you to take the steps you need to overcome the snag in your relationship.

Control your responses. If your partner says something that makes you angry or sad, put those breathing exercises into effect and refrain from flinging out a nasty retort.

Understanding Emotions in Relationships

We all know that it's important to take in and understand your partner's emotions. However, we often forget that we must consider our own emotions as well. Most of us are so used to paying attention to other people's feelings that we don't know how to listen to our own emotions.

Listening to Your Feelings

Knowing how to listen to your feelings is important in having a healthy relationship. For many people, this is a challenge. We live in a world where looking inward and getting in touch with the deeper parts of yourself is not as valued as distracting yourself is. This is largely due to the media and consumerism, where we are constantly bombarded with information, so tuning out of all of this feels nice. Also, we are being sold means of distraction everywhere we go. Looking inward and getting in touch with your feelings will take practice, but it will become easier once you get used to it. There are different ways to do this, and I will outline one of them here for you.

Commit to Doing So

The first step to listening to your feelings is committing to doing so. If you are not committed, it will prove difficult for you to examine yourself without a barrier there. Once you begin listening to your feelings, you will be able to improve the things that are making you feel negative emotions, and the first step to doing this is noticing what those emotions are.

Notice Sensations in Your Body

Once you have committed to looking deep within yourself, you are ready to begin doing so. The best place to start is to notice when something within you feels different. When we feel emotions, we often feel them manifested somewhere in our bodies. Noticing tightness in your chest or a sinking feeling in your stomach usually indicates that you are experiencing some type of emotion.

Give the Feelings a Name

The next step to listening to your feelings after noticing that you feel something is giving that feeling a name. We are all aware of emotions like fear, anger, happiness, surprise, and sadness. These emotions are a good place to begin.

Go Deeper

As we become adults, our emotions become more complex than just the five listed above. We can experience deeper and more complicated emotions, such as shame, anxiety, desperation, shock, doubt, ambiguity, and so on. Once you are comfortable noticing and naming your emotions in a simple way, try to look at them a little deeper and figure out if the emotion you thought was sadness is rather a disappointment.

Listening for Feelings of Your Partner

Once you are comfortable noticing your feelings, giving them names, and then getting deeper into your exploration of them, you will be able to observe and understand the feelings of others more easily. If you cannot understand your feelings, it will prove quite difficult to understand your partner's feelings, even if they put them into words for you. Once you understand the feelings that you experience, you will be able to relate to someone when they tell you that they are feeling anxious, for example, as you may have felt this emotion or something similar as you explored your own emotions.

Chapter 3: Accept Yourself and Your Partner and Strengthen the Friendship

How to Appreciate Your Partner and Accept Them for Who They Are

In any relationship, we need to accept our partners the way they are. No one is perfect and an important thing to remember is that perfection is a myth. No one in this world is perfect and everyone is flawed. If you come into your relationship thinking that your partner is perfect and won't have any issues, you are setting yourself up for very unrealistic expectations. Surprisingly, many enter their relationships with that exact thought in mind and then can't understand why they have issues later on. It's because they didn't realize that chasing perfection doesn't get you anywhere. Instead of making everything perfect, accept your partner how they are and love them unconditionally.

When we decide to share our life with someone else, we've already taken the time to get to know them, and we take the time to understand who they are and what they're about. When we take the step to join our lives with them forever, we have told them that we accept them for who they are. It's after you have gotten in a relationship you find that it isn't true anymore than your relationship needs work. A relationship cannot work if you do not accept your partner for who they are. By that same logic, your partner and yourself will have bad communication and find that you're unable to communicate as efficiently as you'd like to because you feel that your partner doesn't understand you, which can lead to feelings of neglect.

Remember that you don't want your partner to have unrealistic expectations of you so you shouldn't have unrealistic expectations for them, either. If you want your relationship to work, you will need to understand the importance of making sure that you are thinking realistically.

Flexibility is another thing that is going to help you appreciate your partner and make sure that you are accepting them the way they are. It's very easy to think of the world as just black or just white and think that this is wrong, or this is right, and there is no in-between, but that's not realistic. Things don't have to be one way or the other. Instead of labeling your way as the right way or your partner's way as the right way, remember that you need to compromise and understand how things are.

Negative thinking is much easier for some people than positive thinking because being negative doesn't require half as much effort as being positive. When a person is being negative and thinking negatively, it's very self-imposed and self-centered behavior. When we think negatively, we are not accepting our partners for who they are, and instead, you see the negative in them because you're focusing on being negative yourself. Being positive instead of focusing on why your partner is the way he is will cause you to focus on what's amazing about him and why you like him in the first place. In turn, this will lead you to accept him for who he is, and this will lead to you appreciating him for who he is as well. Just as you need the love of your partner to make you happy and whole, your partner needs your love to make him happy and whole as well. He needs you to be here for him as well.

Another helpful hint to appreciating your partner is to force yourself to see things in a different light and put the focus on you. We mean by this that you should ask yourself how you would feel if your partner were judging you the way you're judging them. Another question you should ask is that if they didn't accept you how you're not accepting them, how would you feel if you thought your partner didn't understand you or love you the way you needed to be loved and respected? Keeping this in mind, you'll be much more flexible, and you'll be able to understand why you shouldn't treat your partner this way.

You should also strive to remember that the past is gone and there's nothing you can do about it. You can make up for the past. That part is possible, and we're not saying that it is not. We're saying that whatever happened in the past, you can't go back in time and make it so that didn't happen.

When we judge others, it's often a result of criticisms that we've had to endure ourselves, but we shouldn't put pressure on ourselves to do things a certain way, and we shouldn't put pressure on our partner to do things that way either. Letting what others have said to you or done to you can affect you and your thought process and the way you treat others, including your partner.

When you put unnecessary pressure on your partner, the only thing you're doing is pushing them away. Now, every relationship has pressure, and every relationship has areas where your partner will be under pressure. But what we're saying is, instead of judging yourself and judging others, understand that everyone has limitations. You can't put too much pressure on someone because they will crack.

Something to remember is that even though your partner can meet your needs, you can meet your own needs as well. You can also meet your partner's needs as they meet yours. To fully appreciate your partner and to accept them for who they are, you need to remember that when you are happy with yourself, you'll be happy with everything around you. The same is true if you're unhappy. If you are unhappy with everything around you, you will be overly critical of your partner, and you won't appreciate them for who they are.

When you recognize that you're unhappy, you will at least be able to understand that you need to tell your partner lovingly and respectfully that you're unhappy. Then you can work together on becoming happier so that you can appreciate each other and accept each other the way you need to. Negativity in a relationship is one of the biggest reasons that a relationship can falter. When that happens, it breeds insecurity, painful arguments, and hurt in the relationship you have.

Each of us has to be responsible, at least in part, for our happiness, and because of this, a happy person in a relationship can increase the flexibility and the happiness that you have together as a couple in your relationship. Flexibility is very important when accepting your partner for who he is. When you're able to be flexible, this is the ability to see that you can converse with your partner freely and without judgment. It also helps your ability to be able to compromise in your relationship.

You never want to hurt your partner or be cruel to them, and you need to remember that this is why you need to remember the tips of empathetic dialogue and listening in the same way. The way we speak with our partners can affect every part of our relationship, and if you want to have your partner feel like you appreciate them for who you are, you will need to make sure you watch your words. You can speak to your partner and tell them what you need to say, but there is a proper way to do it and you shouldn't be cruel and unkind.

Let your differences complement each other instead of letting them hurt you. No matter how similar you are in your relationship, you will still have differences. Instead of trying to change your partner or have them try to change you, understand that your differences aren't a bad thing. They can complement you, and they don't have to cause a barrier or a problem for you. Your partner doesn't have to like dancing just because you do or the same television shows. You don't have to hate that your partner doesn't. Let your differences make you stronger and accept that they can work with you and not against you.

Accepting of Your Partner

Release Your Need to Fix Him or Her

Accepting your partner means embracing his or her flaws and imperfections. There is no such thing as a perfect human being. Thus, everyone has some weakness within themselves, regardless of whether they are aware of it. A person must recognize this fact and releases his or her need to fix his or her partner.

Replace Judgement with Compassion

Partners who judge each other always create hostility and conflict in the relationship. The wedge that judgment brings leads to the partners drifting apart and even breaking up ultimately. Replacing a cynical view with compassion enables a person to change perspectives, where they stand in the other person's shoes. A person looking at the situation from his or her partner's perspective allows him or her to appreciate the partner's effort in a challenging moment.

Stop Trying to Control Him or Her

Control tends to stem from a person's conscious or subconscious fear and mistrust. He or she wants his or her partner to act in a way that fits what that person wants. Controlling someone gives a person a sense that he or she has authority over that individual. He or she believes that the decisions made benefit his or her partner and the relationship.

Accept Your Partner for He or She Truly Is

By allowing yourself to release the burden of making your partner your project, tensions will reduce in the relationship. You will get closer to your partner and make him or her feel your respect. Below are inspiring ways to help you learn how to accept your partner for who they are:

Do Not Try to Change Them

It is never a great idea to try changing how someone lives his or her life. Accept your partner for his or her true self and, when necessary, give them ample time to grow and become better. It is also good to realize that people have different maturity levels, especially when there is an age gap. If you are more mature, practice patience and keep guiding your partner to become his or her best version.

Do Not Fuel Your Inner Critic

Most of the time, we tend to put a lot of pressure on ourselves always to do things the right way. Eventually, we end up pressuring others to become to do the same. Not judging yourself too harshly is a great way to start accepting your partner. It helps you to stop extending unnecessary criticism to your partner.

Do Not Compare Your Partner with People from Past Relationships

Another big mistake you can make is comparing your partner with people from your past relationships. Such comparison is one of the most hurtful actions that a person can ever do to their partner. Love your partner just the way he or she is, and do not go looking for a better version of them. Accept things that happened in the past and try moving on. Focus more on your present and future with your current partner. You will not deserve his or her love if you cannot accept the present person you are dating.

Stop Thinking Negatively

It is always easier to look at your partner's negative traits, as it practically requires no effort. When you do not accept your partner for who they indeed are, you will end up concentrating on all the negative traits that he or she possesses. Teach yourself always to see the positive side of someone, such as his or her kindness, calmness, among others. Try fulfilling in yourself what you may find negative about them.

Love Your Partner for What They are on the Inside

You may be tempted to focus on your partner's outward appearances rather than who they are on the inside. For your relationship to be fulfilling, you must learn to know the heart, soul, spirit, mind, personality, smile, and other beautiful things that make your partner unique. It will enable you to experience the happiness that you can share with your partner.

Be Proud of the Achievements and Celebrate Them

Always be proud of your partner's accomplishments and celebrate the person they are now. Develop an interest in his or her past hurdles and any success stories. Compliment your partner as this will help him or her to feel that you are grateful for them. Acceptance starts with being happy for your partner and his or her achievements. You also show the world how proud you are of being his or her partner.

Learn to Love Yourself First

Learning to love and appreciate yourself first is a significant step towards accepting your partner. When you live a happy and fulfilled life, you will be less judgmental towards your partner. Make it your responsibility to love yourself first. When you learn to find your happiness, you will not overburden your partner by being too needy.

Never Judge Your Partner with Their Past

You may find yourself judging your partner for all the mistakes that he or she did in the past. Find it in your heart to forgive him or her for all the past mistakes. Recognize your partner's efforts to change and become a better person. The past may be the reason why your partner is who he or she is now, but it does not define them. Let them know that you accept them for the person they are now.

Make Time to Listen to Your Partner Truly

As the relationship progresses, you may find your partner complaining that you never listen during arguments or general conversations. Listening takes more than just hearing what your partner has to say. Making time to listen to your partner helps him or her to feel that you understand him or her. It lets your partner know that you are not against him or her in any manner, even during the hottest of arguments.

Promise to Love Your Partner Unconditionally

Loving your partner for who he or she truly is a blessing and the aim of lasting relationships. Unconditional love provides a valuable sense of security and happiness, which a person shares with his or her partner. The partner also feels joy from knowing that an individual cares for him or her wholeheartedly. A person accepts and always stands by his or her partner. It is so even when it hurts, or is extremely difficult to do so.

How to Be Yourself Naturally

In any part of life, it is important for you to be yourself and it is very important in a relationship. If you can't be yourself in your relationship, then you have a serious issue. Your partner needs to see you. If you're hiding who you really are, then your partner never knows you. Why then would you stay in a relationship with someone who doesn't truly know you? The answer is simple. You would want a solution. No one wants to stay in a situation where they feel like they don't know their partner.

Some important reasons that being yourself are so important in a relationship are so that your partner can get to know the real you. If your partner doesn't know the real you, then they can feel deceived, hurt, and feel like they're in a relationship with someone who is a fraud or who doesn't understand them at all. They could also feel as if they don't know you at all and everything that they have built-in this relationship is a lie, like you haven't told the truth in any aspect. Another reason this is so important is that your partner wants to know the real you—not an idea of you or a fake persona that you may be using. They want to love you and all of you just the way you are. You should want to be able to be yourself for your partner as well.

When we are hiding who we are and are not acting like ourselves, we begin to put up a fake persona and have people think that is the real us. Like the people that make-believe, they have a great life on Instagram or Twitter. They make their relationship look perfect though it is fake. An interesting thing to note is that hiding yourself can come from fear. The fear is of being able to speak or fear of showing who we really are. When you're trying to communicate in a relationship with your partner, the communication is stifled when you're too afraid to say what you really want to say or you're too afraid to show who you really are. This fear can keep you from recognizing your true self, but it can also severely impact your relationship and the trust and unity the two of you have together. As this would be affecting the communication in your relationship, the communication would break down. As the communication breaks down because of this fear and because you're not honest, your relationship will falter.

A true connection in a relationship should have you and your partner being real with each other. When you can't do this, you keep your partner at arm's length, and you have to hide how you feel and what you want out of your life. Your partner can't relate to you because he doesn't know you. We have spoken about why practicing empathy and why it is important for communication. Being your true self gives your partner the opportunity to relate to you and understand how you're feeling. Without being able to relate to you, he can't do this.

What you need to do for yourself and for your relationship is to be yourself. Your natural self. If you can do this, then your relationship will have the ability to have a relationship that won't be mired in fear and manipulation but trust and love. In order to learn how to be yourself, you need to understand how special you are.

You are a special person, and the first thing you need to do is being able to remember that every day. You have something inside you that makes you different from everyone else around you. This is a great thing! Imagine how boring life would be if we were all the same. You have your own strengths and feelings that make up who you are. Living as yourself means that you're happy with who you are and realizing that you don't have anything to hide and that you can be yourself.

You should also have a hobby that's your own. It is amazing if you share a lot of the same interests and hobbies as your partner, but you should also have a hobby that allows you to do things on your own. Doing things on your own is another thing that you need to do for yourself because this is going to lead to a balance in your relationship. You're still a unique individual that has different wants and tastes than your partner and doing something on your own is a great way to discover who you are if you haven't already. This is also going to help your relationship at the same time.

Going out with your friends or your family can be a really great thing to do for you and yourself as well. If you're not a social type of person, you can talk to people that you care about and that you like hanging out with. Your partner can also do this because they need to have time with their friends as well. If you desire to do this together, you may, but it's just as important that you do it for yourself as well. It's okay to have friends that are just yours.

You need to make sure that you love yourself as well. This is one of the most important tips. You can't truly be yourself if you are not loving yourself. When you don't love yourself, you tend to hide who you really are and tell people what they want to hear. You shouldn't do that. Let them fall in love with the real you. This is going to ensure that you keep things in your life and in your relationship balanced.

You have your own thoughts and ideas, as well as your own wants. You don't need to agree with your partner on everything all of the time. If they're doing something that makes you uncomfortable or if there's even something that you don't like, you need to tell them.

Respect is big in any relationship as well, and if you can't respect yourself, how are you going to respect your partner? Respecting yourself is a key part of being able to accurately and honestly be yourself. If you feel like you are giving more than you can, this isn't healthy for your relationship, but it's also damaging to you and being able to feel any sense of self.

Remember that no one is perfect. Don't try to be the perfect partner for your partner. Perfection is a myth and many couples have hardships because they try to chase the impossible. You won't discover who you are chasing perfection. Admit that it's okay to make mistakes. You don't need to be anything other than yourself because your partner loves you for you are. No relationship is perfect, and if you are able to remember this, then you will be able to have a good relationship and be proud of yourself for who you are. If you have done wrong, admit it and then understand and move on while making sure that you don't repeat that same mistake.

In understanding who you are, you should realize that there are things that you can do and things that you can't. You and your partner need to accept the fact you have limitations. If there is something that you feel like you can't do, then you need to be honest about it and tell your partner that you can't do whatever it is your partner is asking of you.

Keep a good fitness routine. Many people say that when they are discovering who they are, confidence is a big part of discovering who they are. Just as many have said that fitness gave them a large boost in their confidence.

Challenging yourself can also offer great benefits as well. Being able to push yourself and challenge yourself can offer a boost of confidence and push you outside of your comfort zone. Once you've begun to do this, the more success you will have as well as gaining new skills and new virtues or thoughts.

Something that can help you find out who you are is also to take charge of your mental health as well as your physical health. This is going to be able to help you in the long run because it changes how your attitude is.

Personal growth can help you learn who you are and help you to be who you are in your relationship as well. It can also help you find a new sense of self-worth, which allows you to see your relationship, yourself, and your partner with brand new eyes. When people invest in their own personal growth, they can find that they are claiming a part of themselves that they feel like they've lost.

Chapter 4: Intimacy

How to Build Intimacy in a Relationship

Establishing Relationship Commitment

If you intend to increase your emotional intimacy, it should start from within. Understanding what your partner feels is one of the best ways of better establishing your relationship. In order to effectively do this, you should build upon your belief in one another and agree that there are some considerations that you should both adhere to. The following are some of the considerations:

You should practice honesty in your relationship. Being true should not only be in words; more importantly, you should be honest in your actions. You should not be afraid to open up and let your partner know everything about you—how you feel, what bothers you, and why you react to things in a certain way. This will strengthen the emotional link between the two of you.

Exploring Your Partner's Body

In the process of exploring your partner's body, never be afraid to lose yourself momentarily. Devote your time and energy solely for the exploration and you should do it with all the love and enthusiasm you have. This activity is not exclusively for new partnerships—it is also effective for those who have been together for the longest time. Do not be afraid to explore and re-explore each other's body if you want to increase your emotional intimacy.

Maximize Sex Positions

Believe it or not, there are sex positions that can help convert simple sexual intimacy into emotional intimacy. In case you haven't realized it yet, achieving emotional intimacy is more challenging than obtaining sexual intimacy.

Create Intimate Moments Whenever Possible

A man and woman joined together in marriage have the task of getting together, not just because of physical attraction or emotional affection but because of a joint purpose of carving out a loving life together. Your mate is in your life to be with you in this journey called life. You two are to work together to fulfill the same destiny.

Keep on Dating Your Spouse

When was the last time you went on a date with your husband or wife? You may say you went out with your children on a birthday, an anniversary dinner, or perhaps at a wedding. It may also be with your friends on a night out. But when was the last time you were alone as a couple and you two went out just like you did during your early years together?

If you can't remember the last real date you had with your spouse simply to enjoy each other's company, then it's time to change your schedule and approach to spending quality time with one another. Dating shouldn't stop after the sound of the wedding bells or the first cry of the baby.

Encourage One Another

In a world that's filled with negativity, you should be your spouse's number one cheerleader and vice versa. Competition can already be tough at work; plus, modern culture is telling you the countless things you have to possess before you're considered a success. Getting to come home to a supportive spouse is one true blessing indeed.

Most of us are already aware of our flaws. As for those we're not conscious about, we probably already hear enough complaints from our partners and other people in our lives. How often do you truly encourage one another? There is much to be said regarding supportive words. They uplift, inspire, take away blues, boost confidence and strengthen bonds between spouses.

Spice Things Up with a Positive Attitude

When a husband and wife experience conflict, or experience challenges throughout the relationship, it's how they react to it that makes a difference. A negative person can become bitter, or will protect themselves from being hurt again.

Rekindling the romance in a marriage takes commitment and the right mindset. The first step is being positive. You started hopeful about the marriage itself, otherwise, you wouldn't have made the commitment. You and your partner need to believe that things can get better, even after a disagreement. It's not about finding a way out when things get rough. It's not about saying that it was a mistake marrying that person. It's about solving problems - finding solutions, instead of more things to gripe about.

Checking with Each Other Each Day

One thing that most people fail to realize is that even though you spend hours of the day with that special someone, the chances are that you might still not have an emotional and intimate connection with them. However, it is not about the amount of time you spend with each other. The question is, how quality is that time together?

Get to Know Your Partner on a Deeper Level

How do you know your partner more than you already know about them? Someone might say that they already know all they need to know about their spouses, and there is nothing left to know. Well, to be precise, this is not true!

Try New Things

Try to identify some new exciting, terrifying, and exhilarating activities that you and your partner can engage in. When there is a mix of these feelings in those activities, the truth is that they will go a long way in enhancing your attachment to each other. You will realize that there are tons of things you have in common with your spouse that you had no idea existed, and that alone is enough to glue your relationship together.

Solving Intimacy Problems

Identify Your Love Language

Discover how you best show your love to each other. Different partners have different ways of showing affection towards each other. This love language is more vivid in the first few years of your married life.

Exclusively Express Your Concerns About a Certain Problem

When expressing your concerns, be as specific as possible. Make plans together to work towards achieving a reasonable conclusion, even if the problem is minor. Focus on one thing at a time and give all your energies into making sure you get the best out of the things you are getting.

Do Not Doubt the Emotions You Have

Emotions could be wrong but could also be ultimately the interpretation of the true circumstances that affect our physical and mental well-being. Listen to your emotions carefully and interpret them according to other physical factors surrounding your marriage relationship.

If affection is among the things you need emotionally, be open to your partner about it, and tell them exactly what you feel you need. You could acknowledge the fact that they've been trying to give you affection, but you need to indicate that you need more than what you are getting.

Show Your Affection Openly

Affection can be easily cultivated where affection is given. Sometimes you don't need to express your need for some affection, you just need to start showing one in order to be shown one. In fact, most of the things you demand while expressing the need for better intimacy are the exact things you should be doing to yourself and to your spouse.

What Conversations Build Intimacy with Partner?

A lack of love and affection in any form makes the thing less valuable. Even if it is something as simple as baking a cake, if it isn't done wholeheartedly, the results won't be as joyous and comforting. Love is the essence of everything. There's a little dash of it into everything we do and marriage is no different. But like any other thing requires hard work, so does marriage. Intimacy is one aspect of any relationship that allows the partners to be connected to the highest levels. When they get intimate, their mind, body, and soul all connect on another level.

Building intimacy in a relationship is essential. It is what keeps the couple together. It creates moments of passion between them and keeps the attraction alive. It is also healthy as it releases dopamine and oxytocin from the brain, which makes one feel loved and admired. However, many couples don't realize until late that what they have is just a casual physical connection. There are no feelings involved.

So how can you build/bring more intimacy into your relationship? You will be surprised that all you have to do is speak. Some conversations and actions help the partners stay close. From appreciating one another over the little things to asking them about their childhood, many conversations can bring the couple closer and improve their intimacy and connection. Confused?

Play Out Your Fantasies

The best way to build intimacy is to let each other know-how and where to touch. Ask them what their fantasies are and try to play them out to get away from boring, casual intercourse. However, only ask them if you are willing to listen and act upon it. For example, if one partner likes dominance during the act or says, "I like it rough," you should be willing to allow them to experience that with you freely. You both should be open to the other person's ideas without feeling ashamed or less valued. The more interested both partners are to play out their fantasies, the more they will look for chances to get intimate.

Show Gratitude

One of the best ways to build intimacy with your partner is by expressing gratitude for all that they do for you. Even employees leave when they don't feel appreciated or recognized. You can't expect your partner to stay for long, either. We all crave appreciation. Even if you don't have anything grand to be thankful for them, thank them for being there and helping you out with the work. Thank them for their presence, their supportive words, their ability to listen, and much more. Make it a habit to show gratitude towards your partner so they feel more valued and accepted.

Be Supportive

As important is appreciation in any relationship, so is support. If your partner is going through something difficult, such as a health condition, grief, mental trauma, or emotional instability, it is your job as their partner to support them both emotionally and physically. You don't always have to use words, just sitting by their side and letting them know with your actions that you are there for them is appreciable. At times, we all feel weak, like we will just break down any minute. Having the knowledge that someone is there to hold us and help us stand up in case we fall is reason enough to make you come closer to them. It is the same with friends.

Talk About Life Experiences

Many people think that what is in the past should remain there, but it isn't true. If you have a past that keeps hurting you in some manner or keeps showing up in your face from time to time, let your partner know about it. Some people live with unresolved issues from their childhood they still haven't gotten over. These issues can hinder the relationship with your spouse and prevent it from becoming more intimate.

Converse About Self-Improvement

Talking about improving one's self in different areas of your life can also help you reconnect. For instance, if you know that your partner detests some habits of yours, such as eating unhealthy or smoking, or drinking too much, discussing how you would like to change them to be a better partner to them can also earn you some brownie points.

Show Vulnerability

Not everyone is comfortable being vulnerable in front of someone. It takes guts to allow someone to get a close look at who you are. Luckily, it is also the fastest way to build intimacy. Every partner craves to be the most important part of their partner's life. They want to know all about you, your dreams, aspirations, future goals, childhood traumas, and more. Opening up to each other enriches closeness.

Tell Them Why You Love Them

No one ever gets tired of hearing that someone loves them dearly. Those sweet words melt in our ears like butter in a heated pan. Keep telling your partner why you love them often and ask them the same. At first, you may feel like you are just fishing for compliments, but the biggest advantage will be improved intimacy. When partners express their feelings openly and don't shy away from saying that they love their spouse, it just makes everything seem sweeter.

Chapter 5: How to Solve Couple Problems

Common Relationship Problems and How to Solve Them

Appreciation And Acceptance

Appreciation and acceptance are some of the key qualities that make a healthy and functional relationship. In case you would have decided to go to a therapist instead of relying on our guide, the therapist specialized in couples counseling would collect some basic information on you and your partner, as well as take notes on the key points of your relationship. That way, you, your partner, and the therapist would be able to get to know each other better, while the therapist would also work on making you comfortable with opening up on your first session.

Empathy and Understanding Each Other

Empathy is very important as this quality allows us to understand how others feel, even though we might not have experienced that emotion ourselves, thus helping us understand how other people feel, why they feel that way, as well as identify with their emotional experience. If your relationship lacks empathy, you and your partner might be focusing on your own personal emotions instead, i.e. "me," instead of placing the focus on your relationship, i.e. "we." By understanding each other and by developing the skill of empathy towards one another, you will be able to let your partner know that he is not alone and that you can identify with the way he feels. You should expect the same effort in return, while you and your partner may need to practice your empathy by placing yourselves in each other's shoes when listening to what the other has to say about the way they feel and what they think.

Analyze Your Relationship Together

Once the empathy you have for each other is improved and positively established, you can use a similar analysis technique that you used for analyzing your own emotions and the way your partner feels. You will be analyzing your relationship—together. Presuming that you have already mastered the previous two steps, appreciation and acceptance, and empathy and understanding, it should be easier for you to accept negative results as easily as positive aspects of your relationship during the initial analysis. Perhaps the easiest and most effective way of analyzing your relationship would be having your and your partner's opinions individually provided, so both perceptions of your relationship could be taken into consideration.

Practicing Consciousness

Focus on understanding your partner's perspective and show your appreciation for his feelings and opinion— expect nothing less in return. What is important when having a conflict or a disagreement is to be conscious of the situation you are in as well as conscious about the reasons that might have led to the conflicts, your partner's feelings, action, behavior, and emotional reaction. Your partner should follow up with the same factors when it comes to practicing consciousness against your opinion, thoughts, feelings, and behavior. By focusing on each other, you should be able to guess what is wrong as well as learning how to act and react towards finding a possible solution.

Equality Over Inequality

You and your partner are different in many things, which is a perfectly normal and healthy thing, while one shouldn't expect their partner to adopt their opinions, beliefs, and perception—the only thing you may require is understanding your differences and showing appreciation for these same differences as well as similarities you can note between the two of you. These differences are displayed by adopting different roles in the relationship based on individual abilities and skills that your partner and you have. One of you might be better at resolving conflicts, and one of you may be a better listener, and so on. However, these differences should be appreciated in terms of allowing your partner to use their abilities to help the overall improvement of your relationship and overcoming issues and problems you may have in your relationship. You should both encourage mutual and individual expression and identify as equal when it comes to the way your relationship is functioning.

In case you have successfully mastered acceptance, appreciation, empathy, connection and intimacy, consciousness, and equality exercises that means that you and your partner have full support for each other while mutually working on the same goal. The strength of your relationship lies in the fact that you have decided to be there for each other and invest some effort in your relationship in order to stay together and enjoy each other's company.

Unfulfilled Emotional Needs

One of the common reasons behind having a seemingly strong relationship coming to an end is the feeling that one or both partners can have regarding unfulfilled emotional needs. When you don't feel that your emotional needs are being fulfilled it becomes rather difficult to motivate yourself into working on improving your relationship as you may start to believe that your partner doesn't love you or doesn't provide appreciation and recognition for the way you feel. The best way of letting your partner know what you need in order to feel emotionally satisfied is to learn more about your emotional needs in the first place. Make sure to trace your own emotions and analyze your needs.

You can keep a journal and make notes on emotional needs you are able to recognize as necessary for you to feel emotionally fulfilled. Make sure that once you are fully aware of what you need in a relationship, that you are also able to show your needs to your partner, so you could both work on meeting each other's needs. Be prepared to hear your partner's needs as well, and don't be surprised if your partner feels the same. Feeling emotionally unfulfilled may lead to losing connection with your partner, as well as losing touch with the way your partner feels. Both partners should work on recognizing and acknowledging each other's emotional needs in order for the relationship to work. Take care that the feeling of unfulfilled emotional needs that you and your partner may feel is not a product of neediness and codependency, as these emotional needs should be revised towards creating healthier needs that provide both freedom and connection for both partners.

Lack Of Support

In case one of the partners or both of you are expressing behavior that may make the other partner feel like you think you are better than them, while often receiving criticism and disapproval from you, you may be dealing with a lack of support in your relationship. In case your partner is turning to eye-rolling, disregards your opinion, and is often criticizing anything you do, you are probably losing trust in your partner, while intimacy, connection, appreciation, recognition, and validation that should exist in your relationship, is also suffering—this type of behavior consequently leads to completely losing trust in your partner, while it may eventually lead your relationship to an ugly end. You shouldn't be taking your partner's side at all times, especially when you know for a fact that your partner is not right regarding a certain case. However, you should provide support for your partner in terms of being able to show that you are there for them, while also expecting support in return.

Getting Used to Each Other

Getting comfortable with each other will improve your connection and intimacy, but getting used to each other's company may result in a lack of intimacy, simultaneously affecting positive dynamics in your relationship. Positive dynamics means that you and your partner are working on your intimacy by spending free time together, going out, taking a few days off to organize a weekend getaway, having dinner or lunch together, kissing and holding hands, and showing your affection and appreciation in general.

Difficulties with Resolving Conflicts and Problems

The reason why we are often returning to conflicts and disagreements, and ways to resolve these problems, lies in the fact that many couples are struggling with negative communication in terms of being unable to effectively and efficiently resolve their disagreements. As previously discussed, the key to resolving negative communication is establishing equality in the relationship, as well as focusing on understanding your partner's point of view rather than brainstorming on how to defend your own ego from being attacked by your partner. When you decide to give trust and receive trust, you also need to be ready to understand that giving trust means that you will also have confidence in the fact that your partner is not trying to attack you just for the sake of making you feel bad.

Poor Sex Life

Can a couple grow tired of each other in bed? The answer is, probably. In case you and your partner are failing at making an effort to show your partner that you are attracted to them and that you care, your sex life may be suffering. Many studies conducted on couples indicate that dissatisfactory sex life is one of the main problems people encounter in relationships, causing a breakup after causing a loss of connection, intimacy, and passion. You and your partner may feel the lack of chemistry and attraction between you, which may appear as a result of being together for a long time in a relationship with poor dynamics.

Inability to Comply with Changes in Your Relationship

We are all inclined towards constant and periodic changes, while changes in form of changing life stages represent perfectly normal progress in anyone's life. Sometimes, as we are changing, the way we observe others and relationships with other people likewise change as a consequence. During our personal development and individual changes, our partners' changes occur simultaneously, while it may occur that the way we changed doesn't match the idea of change noted in our partner's individual metamorphosis. Although you are both still the same people, you can notice that your necessities are changing as your relationship is developing, which may bring issues to your relationship in case you and your partner are not able to comply with these changes.

Allowing External Factors to Affect Your Relationship

We are all vulnerable to external factors and outside stressors at times or frequently as we are managing multiple important aspects of our life—job, kids, home, finances, friends, family, and relationship you have with your partners. Not all these aspects will appear to be functional at all times, which is the time when we become more vulnerable to external stress factors. While life may create many scenarios that have the ability to put you in distress, your relationship shouldn't be affected by these factors in case you have a strong base in your relationship.

Infidelity And Betrayal

Trust, honesty, support, intimacy, connection—all these qualities may fall under the negative influence of infidelity, directly disturbing the foundation of your relationship. Although considered to be a "cardinal sin" when it comes to relationship commandments, consequences from infidelity and betrayal can be worked through if the couple is ready to forgive and accept the fact that people change for better and for worse likewise. If both partners agree that infidelity is something that can be forgiven, the couple may continue working on retrieving trust and practicing honesty.

Differences in Parenting Methods

When it comes to married couples, who had become parents, and couples with children, conflicts may arise due to the differences in parenting methods. It is difficult to come to an agreement when your philosophies on how to raise a healthy and happy child are different. However, this is something that needs to be done—not only in order to preserve the peace in your relationship and in your family but to make sure that you are able to provide a healthy and constructive environment for your child. Agreement and planning are the key strategies in this case, as both partners need to overcome their differences in this case and think of what is best for the child from an objective point of view. "What is best for the child" may sometimes be used as an excuse by one of the parents (partners) to manipulate the other parent into accepting their own perception and philosophy on how to take care of the family and your child—this sort of behavior is negative and can be considered as a way of manipulating. One should never use a child in order to impose their set of values.

Chapter 6: How to Behave During Conflicts

Common Causes of Conflict

There are quite a few stressors in our everyday lives that can trigger an argument with the ones we love most. What are those stressors, and how should we resolve the issues that arise with our partners? Let's find out.

Financial trouble is one of the most common triggers for a fight in a relationship. There are different scenarios as to how it gets started. The two of you do not agree on how and when to spend your money, you can't decide who pays for what on a date, or one of you has recently lost a job and the other person feels distressed about being the sole breadwinner. It is understandable that this can cause a ton of stress, but fighting about it does not provide a solution. You need to sit down and plan ahead of time how to spend your finances, who pitches in for a certain bill or date, and a contingency plan for being fired. When you know ahead of time what you can do in a period of confusion or tough situations, the weight will surely be lifted off of your shoulders.

Moving causes an immense amount of stress in couples. Both parties must agree on a place to live, whether moving is best for each person's work life and when the moving should be done. Then there is the sweaty, hard work that comes with packing and unpacking. The whole ordeal is exhausting, and tensions rise when people are tired. In this case, plan far ahead. You can't always know when you might have to move, of course, but talk about what both of you want from each area far before you ever think of moving for real. That way, when the time comes, you will already have a good idea of what to look for. If you need to, write everything down and review it when the time comes.

A lack of intimacy, sexually or otherwise, is frustrating. If you are a person who is interested in sex or want to be affectionate and your partner isn't as forthcoming with it, you feel put out and unattractive. The best thing to do for this sort of problem is to be honest with your partner about your feelings. How are they supposed to know they are not meeting your needs if you never tell them?

Politics and religion. These are firmly-held core beliefs that indicate the views that a person considers to be of utmost value. Ideally, you two would have discussed these topics before you decided to be exclusive or get married. If you never got around to it and those things are coming up now, settle your differences by talking to each other about *why* these beliefs are so important to you and what they mean about how you want to live your lives. Do not try to convert each other; that is the biggest no-no of all. When you preach to your partner and try to get them to act like you, you are telling them that their beliefs are less important than your own. If you want any sort of peace, you must have a mutual understanding and agree to let your significant other be who they want to be. If the way they act due to their political or religious standings is unbearable, use this book to help you with your new partner when the time comes.

Stay optimistic and reach a compromise. Both of you may have a different end-goal to the conversation in your mind, and you'll be severely disappointed when you do not end up getting what you want. If you have to compromise, I promise it will not be the end of the world. Your relationship is by no means doomed just because your beloved would like to go out with her friends more often and leave you at home to your own devices. Instead of pouting about it, reach a mutual decision to set how many days per week you are comfortable with her doing so, and give in a little to meet her needs for other social interaction—negotiate.

How to Manage Conflicts

The most complicated and confusing thing to successfully manage in a relationship is a conflict. Tensions run high, and at the moment, you both say things you shouldn't to try and "win" the argument. You end up regretting it later, but some things cannot be taken back. It is a challenge for all couples, even those who have been together for decades. It's never too late to change your bad habits using the skills we've already talked about and the advice here. Shall we continue? I think so if you want to keep your love alive.

Setting the Right Environment

There must be some level of security and trust in your relationship before you can even begin to talk about the rough stuff with your partner. If you have hidden important information from them in the past or have been cruel during previous arguments, you have to put in some effort to regain that level ground you two were on in the beginning. The most important ways to create a calm and safe space are fairly simple. You just have to know where to start and what to do.

Trust

The best time to begin gaining the trust of another person, especially a romantic interest, is right away. No relationship is going to last long if, after a month, you still haven't done anything to deserve unwavering belief. How do you go about building it, though? It's elementary!

Never assume that anyone is going to trust you without a bit of work on your part. Earn it—stick to what you say you will do and do it! If you consistently prove that your promises are sincere, you'll gain the trust of your partner.

What to Do if You've Broken Your Partner's Trust Before

After you lie to someone, you may find yourself wondering what compelled you to do such a thing. This can be scientifically explained, though it isn't an excuse to continue with bad behavior.

The first step to regaining trust is to acknowledge both to yourself and verbally to your partner that you did something wrong. Apologize in a sincere way. Your apology is not coming from the right place if you shrug the blame onto them for your actions. Half-apologies like, "Sorry you feel the way you do," or "Sorry, I didn't mean to/I didn't know" are unacceptable. It is not about making excuses for yourself. It's about what you did to your partner. The way you word it is important; make amends by validating the other person's feelings.

You may want to assure them that you will never betray their trust again; don't. If they already doubt you, they are not going to believe in your promises. Let your actions speak for you in the future. Be better by avoiding the situations and people that encourage or tempt you to lie to your partner. Anyone who wants to get in the way of what you have is *not* a real friend.

Be patient and give your relationship time to grow. You won't get results overnight, but you will get them sooner if you start now and keep building that trust and faithfulness consistently.

How to Restore Balance in a Relationship

Resolving an argument with your significant other? Is that even possible? Won't they just keep bringing it up from time to time? Have you ever met my spouse?

Well, the truth of the matter is that settling an argument is fairly easy when both the partners acknowledge the differences in opinions and are ready to address the issues decently. We shall discuss more on this in Part 3, but for now, let's learn some foolproof means not only to end an argument but settle it once and for all.

Focus on the Present

Arguments are the result of unsettled conflicts from the past. However, trying to bring up something entirely different from what you two are fighting about will only add to the resentment you two have. Avoid doing that and focus on the current issue only. This also goes for all those times when you try to use that past to prove a point or convey a message. If anything, it can make your partner feel attacked or judged and shift attention from the present issue.

Personalize Your Statements with "I"

Use sentences that emphasize more a personalized experience rather than a general one. For instance, if you felt insulted when your partner joked about your weight in front of his friends, instead of saying something like, "It's disrespectful when you joke about my weight with our guests," say something like, "I felt so disrespected when you joked about my weight in front of your friends. I felt humiliated."

Use Suitable Language

Never use derogatory language during an argument as it will do anything but settle it. The words you choose and the way you deliver them are very important in any fight with your partner. You may have a different body language that counters your words. Even when you are in a heated conversation, use appropriate language to express your emotions. You have to stay respectful and ensure that your partner doesn't feel disrespected either. This means that you aren't allowed to name-call them as labels can sting you back in the ass the next time you fight with them.

Openly Communicate Your Expectations

Be clear about what you expect what your partner needs to do. No need to confuse them with riddles or avoid conversing with them just because they did something that you didn't like. Sometimes, our words can also have double meanings or be understood in different manners, which is why it is always best to be crystal clear about your expectations when settling an argument with your partner.

Reach Out for Support

If the issue doesn't reach a fruitful conclusion still, maybe you need someone else to intervene and take over. Sometimes, a new perspective can help both partners see the problem from a completely different angle. This is where professional counseling or therapy comes in. Hire a marriage counselor to improve communication. A professional counselor may help you with tips on how to talk to each other without riling up or how to resolve arguments and conflicts.

Conclusion

Thank you for reading this book. I genuinely hope it has offered you multiple strategies about communicating with your spouse to lay the foundation of a lasting, happy, and fulfilling relationship.

A little bit of understanding and effort can go a long way in fixing even the biggest of issues. You have to understand that your relationship should be a source of strength and happiness for both you and your partner. You should both be able to freely express yourself and be assured of validation when you need it. It's not about agreeing on all things, even when you disagree. Instead, it's about picking your fights and expressing yourself in the right way.

If you've just had a challenging situation in the relationship, it may not improve immediately. It may be a slow process that needs more time, effort, and attention to grow into a strong and indestructible bond gradually.

Unfortunately, most people tend to enter into relationships with no idea of what they are hoping to achieve or gain from the relationship. Without an idea of what they want or a sense of purpose, people can feel frustrated and aimless. Fortunately, it is never too late to do the smart thing and create a good relationship vision.

Friendship involves expressing mutual care, compassion, and trust between friends. It indicates that a person shares values with someone else and deliberately chooses to invite him or her into his or her life.

Caring means being kind and showing concern. Affection is a feeling of fondness and endearment to a person or place. It is a tangible way of showing that a person is fond of someone. Caring and affection, therefore, give the idea of a person showing kindness and concern for people whom he or she is fond of.

Accepting your partner means embracing his or her flaws and imperfections since there is no such thing as a perfect human being. Therefore, everyone has some weakness within himself or herself, regardless of whether he or she is aware of it or not. A person must recognize this fact and releases his or her need to fix his or her partner and accept him or her just as he or she is.

Empathy is the ability to understand and feel with someone else. Being empathetic is having the ability to get into the shoes of another person and feel what he or she is feeling as if you are going through a certain experience with him or her.

To discover your love language, you need to observe and be keen on the way your partner expresses his or her love to you. Take note of what you are always complaining about and what he or she does that you like. By analyzing both situations, you get to discover your love language.

Let this guide help you to find your own path to succeed in your relationship. Let this help you work out the differences you two have. Let it show you how to handle criticism, conflicts, and arguments. Let it tell you how to appreciate, communicate and love more deeply. Let it make way for you to forgive when wronged and rebuild with a clean slate.

And most importantly, let it teach you how to communicate with your spouse on a secondary level without any fear of rejection, judgment, or failure. The only failure is not expressing emotions and feelings openly, so don't make that mistake.

Allow the relationship to blossom by contributing in your tiny ways to make your spouse feel special. Chalk out an arrangement beforehand about tackling conflicts and disagreements. Listen, and think about the other person while attempting to resolve differences. Keep an open communication and objective mindset approach.

Good luck.

CPSIA information can be obtained
at www.ICGtesting.com
Printed in the USA
BVHW090334220621
610126BV00012B/2649